FAQ
TEEN LIFE™

FREQUENTLY ASKED QUESTIONS ABOUT

Budgeting and Money Management

Matt
Monteverde

ROSEN
PUBLISHING®

New York

Published in 2009 by The Rosen Publishing Group, Inc.
29 East 21st Street, New York, NY 10010
www.rosenpublishing.com

Library of Congress Cataloging-in-Publication Data

Monteverde, Matt.
Frequently asked questions about budgeting and money
management / Matt Monteverde. — 1st ed.
    p.cm.—(FAQ: Teen Life)
Includes bibliographical references and index.
ISBN-13: 978-1-4042-1804-8 (library binding)
1. Budgets, Personal—Juvenile literature. 2. Teenagers—Finance,
Personal—Juvenile literature. I. Title.
HG179.M596 2009
332.024—dc22

                                                2007045355

Manufactured in the United States of America

Contents

one

WHY IS BUDGETING IMPORTANT?

For many people, the idea of budgeting their money is about as appealing as dieting. But diets often tell you exactly what to eat, whereas budgets do not tell you exactly how to spend your money. A budget is a plan that is used by both individuals and businesses. A personal budget is used to help you live as well as possible with the money that you have. In the business world, budgets help managers plan as well as possible for their companies and employees.

One of the largest budgets you hear about is that of the United States government. It is called the federal budget, and it is designed to keep track of how the government spends its money and collects its income (taxes and other revenues). Currently, the federal budget is unbalanced. This occurs in a budget when too much money is spent or not enough money is received. The result of an unbalanced budget is that there is

A budget is basically a plan in numbers. With a good budget, you know where your money is coming from as well as where it is going.

not enough money to pay all of the bills. In order to balance the federal budget, members of the Congress pass measures regulating how funds are spent.

It is obvious that a government needs to have a budget and keep track of how its money is spent and received. But what if you don't work and have only a small allowance from your parents? Even if you don't have a lot of money to keep track of, there are still good reasons to learn budgeting skills. A budget can help you in several ways. When you start college and begin to live on your own, it will become increasingly important to manage your personal budget and to know the fundamentals of spending. The decisions you make about spending now will prepare you for when you become an independent adult. Therefore, it's smart to start thinking about it now!

Knowing Where and How You Spend Your Money

A recent study showed that American teens spent more than $169 billion in 2004. It also showed that teens spend most of their money on clothing (33 percent) and food (21 percent). Entertainment items such as movies, CDs, and games are other popular products that teens spend their money on. While it can be fun to spend money on entertainment and recreation, it is also important to budget money. Using a budget to keep track of money may decrease the worries of many people. That is because budgeting can help you have a feeling of control over your money.

Setting Aside Money for Bills

Comparing families in industrialized countries, Americans have one of the lowest rates of savings per household. A budget can't make a person save money, but it can help. Also, a budget will increase the chances that money is spent in a wise fashion.

Perhaps you currently receive an allowance from your parents or hold a part-time job after school. By budgeting the

If you budget wisely, you will be able to pay for the things you need while still being able to afford the things you want—like a fashionable new purse.

money that you receive each week, it may be possible for you to pay for what you need, such as lunches, bus fare, and clothing, and still save for things you want, such as video games or designer clothing. Apart from setting money aside for your wants, budgeting helps ensure that you will have money set aside for necessities like food, rent, and bills.

Preparing for Unforeseen Expenses

Suppose you borrow a friend's in-line skates for the weekend. While skating, one of the wheels catches on a rock and pulls loose from the boot. Your friend agrees to wait while you have the wheel replaced, but where will you get the money to pay for the repair?

If you budgeted your money effectively, you might have some money set aside for unforeseen expenses, such as the

Do you work a part-time job to earn your spending money? Having a budget will help you protect your hard-earned income.

broken skate. Other common unforeseen expenses include car repairs and medical bills. As your personal income and expenses grow over time, the ability to adjust and maintain a budget will enhance your personal and professional life.

An Increasingly Important Skill

As we have entered the twenty-first century, increased knowledge and skills are required to compete in the changing workplace created by the world economy. The use of budgets is one of the most important skills to have in the new millennium. Allocating money, solving problems, and making decisions are skills needed to create and use either a personal or business budget. These skills are also critical for people who want to be ready to achieve personal and professional success.

If you learn good budgeting skills and are able to apply them to different situations, people will take notice. At your current job, you can impress your employer by suggesting possible budgeting improvements. If you help your boss now, he or she will likely help you later. Maybe your boss will write you a good recommendation for a future job. Or perhaps he or she will even help you find a better job when you finish school. Whatever the case, using your budgeting skills now can only benefit you in your future career.

Balancing your current budget, no matter how little money it may involve, will help you balance your personal budget in the future. You will be making more money when you begin your career, but balancing your budget then will involve the same

Learn money management skills when the numbers are smaller. It will make it easier to budget when you get older and your income and expenses increase.

steps that it does now. That way, when you do begin to earn more money—and possibly even have to balance a budget that includes a spouse and children—you will be well prepared to do it.

Success with budgets can be achieved. Many people start with basic personal budgets when learning to budget money. Tracking budget items and adjusting the budget over time gives experience that can be used with more complex budgets. Budgeting your allowance prepares you to budget when you have income from a job, for example. And budgeting part-time earnings prepares you to budget for your own business someday.

A budget may not make you rich. However, when used with creativity, budgets can provide a sound basis on which to make decisions that will be easy to live with. Even if you don't have a lot of money to keep track of, there are still good reasons to learn budgeting skills.

two

WHAT ARE THE BUDGETING BASICS?

Many people believe that creating and using a budget is about as much fun as going to the dentist. But using a budget doesn't have to be an anxiety-filled chore. Budgeting is a process of organization that helps people to realize their financial goals and dreams. Four basic steps are followed in organizing a budget:

1. Setting financial goals.
2. Determining income.
3. Figuring expenses.
4. Subtracting expenses from income.

Setting Financial Goals

A goal is a target that you set for yourself, something that you want to achieve. Goals can be large, such as saving for a car, or small, such as finding babysitting jobs to increase your income. Whether large or small, it is important to know your goal.

It may be helpful to think of your budget as a road map. It will mark the route from your current financial situation to a goal down the road. Like a map, there may be various paths that you can take to your goal. Studying your map, you can find the shortest one.

To understand where your budget can take you, first determine your goals in budgeting. Ask your parents about their financial goals. Do they use a budget? If not, why? Ask a few friends about their goals and how they plan to achieve them.

If your parents seem to be good at tracking income and expenses, ask them to show you how they manage the family budget.

Next, divide your wishes into two groups: short-term goals and long-term goals. That will help you decide which to work on first. Short-term goals are smaller goals, things that can be accomplished in a short time, around six months to a year. Long-term goals are larger projects that take longer than a year to achieve. One short-term goal might be saving up some cash to purchase a new video game system, while a long-term goal might be saving up for college tuition, or buying a car or truck.

Determining Your Income

A budget tracks how much money is received (income) and how much money is spent. To start using a budget, you must know how much money you have or will receive. Make a list of all the ways that you receive money. Even if you currently have only one source of income, it is important to list it. Your list may include:

- Allowance
- Gifts from relatives
- Babysitting fees
- Odd jobs such as car washing or lawn mowing

If you work or have multiple sources of income, you may want to create a worksheet to illustrate your sources of income. As your income grows, a worksheet can also help to track income that your savings creates, such as interest income.

Figuring Your Expenses

A budget can allow you to predict whether or not future expenses, or the amount of money that is spent each month, will increase or decrease. But before a budget can be set up, current expenses, or how money is spent today, must also be determined.

Keep a Spending Diary

An easy way to determine current expenses is to record in a diary everything that you spend for a week. This "spending diary" may be nothing more than a slip of paper on which you record every purchase you make. At the end of the week, categorize all the purchases made.

Next, add expenses that occur once a month, such as rent or your cell phone bill. To determine how much you spend weekly on these fixed expenses, divide monthly expenses by four (since there are four weeks in a month). So if in one month, your cell phone bill is $40, and you spend $20 on food, and $20 on clothes, then your total monthly expenses would be $80 ($40 + $20 + $20). If you divide your total monthly expenses ($80) by 4, you will see that your weekly expenses add up to $20 per week.

Some sample categories of expenses are as follows:

- Entertainment, such as books, magazines, movies, DVDs, or compact discs
- Food, such as school lunches and snacks
- Gas money for your car, or car payments (including insurance and repairs)

With a carefully planned budget, you'll know right away whether you can afford tickets to that blockbuster movie you want to see.

➡ Other forms of transportation such as bus or subway fare if you live in a big city and rely on public transportation to get to school and work

➡ Personal care, such as haircuts and cosmetics

➡ Clothing

➡ School/hobby supplies

➡ Cell phone bills

A spending diary is a useful tool if you are just beginning a budget. It is also helpful if you have very few expenses. But it may not be enough if you have many expenses or want to create a monthly budget.

For larger budgets, such as monthly or yearly budgets, many people use a file folder with pockets. Each pocket is labeled with the name of the type of expense, such as "Entertainment" or "Food." Receipts for items purchased during the month are filed in the appropriate pocket. If you buy something without receiving a receipt, simply file a note in the correct pocket. At the end of the month all expenses will be organized and ready to record in your budget.

Use Your Computer Skills

If you're computer-savvy, you can avoid notes, papers, and file folders altogether. Just electronically scan all your receipts or pay stubs to keep digital files of your financial records. Then use a computer program to organize your expenses. Most operating systems come with a spreadsheet program included, like Microsoft Excel in the Windows operating system. Using such programs, you can set up a simple grid that stores and tracks your financial information. All you need to get started is three simple column headers: Income, Expenses, and Total. You can then use the "Formula" feature to automatically calculate your total every time you add a new income or expense. If you're new to using a spreadsheet, formulas can be a little complicated. If you aren't sure how to add a formula to your spreadsheet, use the program's "Help" feature, or ask someone for assistance. As you keep adding to your spreadsheet, the more comfortable you will be using the program, and the better it will fit your needs.

Using a Checkbook

Another good way to help track your spending is in your checkbook. Some people obtain their first checkbook when they are teenagers. If you do not have a checkbook, you will need to get one in the future. A checkbook is a ledger of your transactions, either money being put in or taken out of your checking account. There is a good chance that when you pay your cell phone or credit card bills among others, you will be sending each company a check. After you write out a check, you should write a record of the check's amount, date, and who it is made out to in your checkbook. This will allow you to monitor how much money you have in your checking account. That way you can pay bills and budget accordingly. Here are six simple steps that will help you fill out your checks correctly:

Step 1: Write the date in the upper right-hand corner.

Step 2: Write the name of the store or person to whom you are writing the check on the "Pay to the order of" line.

Step 3: Write the amount of the check—spelled out. For example, for a $25.50 check you would write: "Twenty-five and 50/100."

Step 4: Write the amount in numbers inside the box next to the dollar sign. The box is located next to where you wrote out the amount, in step 3.

Step 5: Write a memo or account number on the memo line. For example, you could write something like "Brakes for car."

Step 6: Sign your full name on the signature line.

Numbers at the bottom of a check include a bank routing number and your checking account number, among others. These help banks move money to and from the right accounts.

Many companies, such as Verizon, also allow you to pay your bills online. Online bill paying offers the convenience of paying your bills without mailing a check. Instead of a check, you can sign up online and have money automatically deducted from your checking account in order to pay bills. If you sign up for such a program and have money taken out of your account, make sure you make a note of the transaction in your checkbook. Also, after paying a bill online, keep the confirmation e-mail you receive, just in case anything goes wrong with the payment.

Subtracting Expenses from Your Income

The fourth and final step in creating a budget is to subtract expenses from income. The result of this process will be either a positive number or a negative number. A positive result shows that income is larger than expenses, whereas a negative result shows that more money is being spent than earned. When the amount of income is equal to or greater than the amount of expenses, a budget is said to be "balanced."

Once You Have a Budget

Setting goals, determining income, figuring expenses, and finding a balance are the four steps for creating a beginning budget. But using these steps to create a budget is not the end of budgeting.

Budgeting is a tool. It is a means of figuring out how much you earn and how much you spend. Once you have determined your financial goals, added up your income, added up your expenses, and then calculated the difference between them, you can see how you spend your money. When you understand how you spend your money, you can decide if you need to change your earning and spending habits in order to reach your financial goals. For example, one of your financial goals may be to save money for a Sony PlayStation. Once you figure out your budget, you might decide you want to set aside $10 per week to help you reach your financial goal. A budget can help you figure out how much money you can save each month—in this case $40, if you put aside $10 each week. That means if a Sony PlayStation costs about $200, it would take you five months to save enough money for the PlayStation.

What if your budget amount at the end of the month is positive? That means that you earn more money than you spend. You may want to earn or save even more, however. Or you may decide that you are already earning enough money to buy something you have been hoping to buy.

What if your budget amount at the end of the month is negative—more money was spent than was earned? Can a budget with a negative balance be fixed? The answer is yes. To change your budget from a negative balance to a positive balance means that you must increase how much you earn or decrease how much you spend. Your budget will help you decide if there are some expenses you can cut or if you need to find a way to earn more money. For instance, perhaps you can buy one compact disc instead of two each month. Or you might offer to rake leaves on the neighbor's lawn or get a part-time job.

Most negative budgets require a month or two of adjustments before they will come into balance. The basic remedies for unbalanced budgets are to reduce spending or increase income. Budget adjustments seem to be the hardest part of maintaining a budget. After all, no one likes to be told to spend less or find an extra job. But with practice and a little creativity, budget adjustments and using budgets in everyday life can be a simple way to achieve financial goals.

Credit Cards

Visa, MasterCard, American Express: These are credit cards, and just about everyone wants one. You see people use them in movies and on television, in magazines, and in real life. People see something they want, and with a credit card, they get it. The message from the credit card companies seems to be: Don't worry about paying for it today; you'll pay for it tomorrow, and the day after tomorrow, and the day after that. That's the problem. Put it on plastic, and you may end up paying four or five times more tomorrow than you would if you had just paid cash today.

The reality is that credit cards are not magic, and they are not free. They are loans, and loans must be paid back. If you do not

With a widely accepted credit card, you don't have to carry around large amounts of cash. This convenience can make shopping a more enjoyable experience.

pay them back, there are serious consequences that can hurt you in the future. If used correctly, however, credit cards can be a helpful tool in budgeting successfully.

Teenagers and Credit Card Use

Many people get their first credit card when they are teenagers. A 2005 survey revealed that one out of three high school seniors uses credit cards, and half are in their own names. When a credit card is in your own name, that means that you are the only one that signs the credit card contract. In order to get a credit card in your own name, you must be eighteen years or older. If you are under eighteen, you can still get a credit card, but you will need a cosigner. Teenagers mainly use their parents as cosigners. A cosigner is someone who along with the applicant signs the credit card contract. Along with the primary borrower (you if you applied for a credit card), the cosigner accepts responsibility for repaying a debt to the credit card company.

Quite often teenagers get credit cards so they can build a strong credit history. It is a good idea to do this because you will need a good credit history in the future when you decide to buy a car or house, or apply for a loan from a bank. If you are not careful though, you can ruin your credit. Unfortunately, this happens to many people when they get their first credit cards.

In 2005, the bankruptcy rate for those under twenty-five years old was higher than 5 percent. These people often get into financial trouble as early as their teenage years, when they obtained their first credit card. To avoid financial trouble, you should realize that with a credit card comes great responsibility. In order to be responsible with your card, it is important to know how to use your card and how to use it carefully.

How to Use (and Misuse) a Credit Card

To get a credit card, you must sign a contract with a bank or another lender, sometimes a store. The credit card company promises to loan you a limited amount of money when you use the card. In return, you promise to pay back the amount you borrowed, plus interest. Interest is what the credit card company charges you to borrow the money, and it can add up fast.

Using credit cards can be very tempting because they allow us to think in terms of monthly payments, instead of how much something really costs at the moment of purchase. Maybe you can't afford to buy a $3,000 item up front, but you think you can afford to pay $30 a month. Let's say you see an incredible, top-of-the-line computer system that you absolutely "must" have. It's $3,000. You don't have that kind of cash but decide to buy it with a credit card and pay it off a little every month.

If you carry a $3,000 balance on a credit card with a 19 percent interest rate and pay the required minimum balance of 2 percent or $15 each month, whichever is less, it would take you thirty-six years to pay off the loan. That's because the minimum payment barely covers the cost of interest. And, what is worse, when you finally pay off that computer after thirty-six years, you will have paid about $9,300 in interest charges alone. That means you will have paid a total of $12,300, which is more than four times the cost of the $3,000 computer. OK, so maybe you have no plans to spend $3,000 all at once. But people can also run up credit card

Because of the way interest rates work, it's smarter to save up and pay cash for an expensive item—like a hot electric guitar—rather than purchasing it using your credit card.

bills quickly just by making smaller purchases, which with interest can add up quickly, and therefore put you in heavier debt than you had intended.

While credit cards can be a one-way ticket to debt, if used carefully, they can be helpful tools. They can get your car fixed in an emergency when you are away from home, or they can help you buy something that you need today but can't afford to pay cash for all at once. In addition, credit card companies will often help you when you are not happy with the product or service you purchased from a merchant. Also, if you use a credit card wisely, you will build a strong credit history. Credit history is a record of your financial responsibility, and banks and other lenders will consider that history when you apply for a loan to buy a house or a car.

Credit Card Companies Want You!

When you are old enough to get a credit card of your own, credit card companies start to send you applications—lots of applications. While it might seem very thoughtful of them to want to help you get those things you've always wanted but could never afford, keep in mind that you are being targeted. Credit card companies love it when teenagers get credit cards. Why? Because some teens don't understand how credit cards work and start buying more than they should on credit. Companies keep very close tabs on the spending habits of their customers. The more you buy using a credit card, the more interest you are forced to pay. Credit card companies want you to spend more than you can afford to spend because if you do, they make more money! They may even try to charge you a higher interest rate. Don't fall for it. Read credit card applications carefully and don't accept an offer that seems too good to be true. Check with your parents or a trusted financial advisor before signing any credit card agreement.

Credit Card Scams

Unfortunately, there are many credit card scams around today. With the rise of the Internet, credit card fraud is probably more common now than ever before. Some people send e-mails requesting your credit card number. It is important not to respond to these e-mails. Also, be very careful about giving out

YOUR CREDIT REPORT

Name: Abacommon, Michael
Address: 1 Apartment COMPLIANT DR 14
City/State/Zip: TOMMORROW IL 60750

Report #: 10239730

Report Date: 2004-02-24

CREDIT INFORMATION

This section lists the consumer's credit accounts - as reported by the three bureaus. It includes the date when those accounts were opened, payment history, debt owed and any co-signers. Watch out for accounts that are not familiar—these could be accounts that were opened fraudulently in your name.

See Creditor Contact Information below

Account: IBC   **Acct #:** 505624730013   **Type:** Credit Card

Bureau	Tradeline Type	Date Open	High Limit	Mo. Pmnt.	Acct. Bal.	Last Reported	Account Status	Amount Past Due
TUC	Individual	2002-02-01	$16700	$497	$0		Open	$0

Bureau	30	60	90+	History Date	24 Month History
TUC	0	0	0	2002-04-01	

Account: MARINE MIDLAND BANK   **Acct #:** 93504XXXX   **Type:** Auto Loan

Bureau	Tradeline Type	Date Open	High Limit	Mo. Pmnt.	Acct. Bal.	Last Reported	Account Status	Amount Past Due
XPN	Individual	1995-12	$2000	$0	$0		Closed	$0

Bureau	30	60	90+	History Date	24 Month History
XPN	0	0	0	1995-12	

Account: ATTWSNEPCS   **Acct #:** 2500000038880XXX   **Type:** Unknown

Bureau	Tradeline Type	Date Open	High Limit	Mo. Pmnt.	Acct. Bal.	Last Reported	Account Status	Amount Past Due
EFX	Individual	2003-09	$0	$0	$0	2003-10	Open	$0

Bureau	30	60	90+	History Date	24 Month History
EFX					

Lenders and credit card companies review credit reports to learn about an individual's history of borrowing and repaying loans.

your credit card number. Don't give out your credit card number over the phone, unless you make the call and know that the company is reputable.

Here are some tips to make sure your credit card information does not get stolen:

- Try not to let your credit card out of sight when you use it, and make sure you get it back as quickly as possible.
- Never provide your credit card information on a Web site that is not a secure site.
- Never leave your credit card or receipts lying around.
- Open your credit card bills promptly and make sure there are no unusual charges that you did not make.
- If you see charges on your bill that you did not make, call your credit card company immediately to report possible fraudulent charges.
- If you lose your credit card, call the company immediately to report it lost.
- If you pay any bills online or receive any financial statements via e-mail, change your passwords every few months.
- If you discard any mail from your credit card company, make sure all personal information, even your address, is unreadable.

Savings Accounts

One of the most reliable methods for saving money is to open a savings account. While checking accounts give you fast access

An account manager at your local bank will be happy to tell you about the different accounts you can open to start earning interest on your savings.

to your money, savings accounts hold on to money you may not need right away. Your money is safer in the bank than it would be if you stored it at home. And the best part is that your savings earns interest.

Earning Interest

Interest can seem like money for nothing. It is the percentage of your savings that the bank pays you for the right to hold your money. You might ask: If they pay me to keep my money, how do they stay in business? Banks take your money and combine it with other depositors' money. Then they can loan this money to borrowers, who typically pay higher interest rates than what the banks pay out on their savings accounts.

As the amount of money in your savings account increases, you earn more interest. Most banks don't require a minimum balance, so you can open a savings account with a very small amount of money. The best way to get started is to check out interest rates at different banks in your area. Most banks have a Web site where you can look up interest rates and savings options before you even visit the bank. Don't be afraid to call and ask questions. Banks want the responsibility of keeping your money for you. Look for banks that are members of the Federal Deposit Insurance Corporation (FDIC). Accounts at these banks are insured by the federal government. So, in the rare case that the bank goes out of business, you are guaranteed to get your money back, up to $100,000. It's also a good idea to keep your money at a bank where the employees are friendly and helpful.

How Does Interest Work?

A typical savings account can earn anywhere from 1 percent to 4 percent interest. There are two different kinds of interest: simple interest and compound interest. With simple interest, extra money is generated based on the amount of the original sum of money. For instance, let's say you put $100 in a savings account with a 4 percent simple interest rate. Assuming that your interest is calculated every year, you will earn $4 every year. With compound interest, you earn more money because the amount of interest you have already earned is factored in with the original sum.

In other words, after ten years, with a 4 percent simple interest rate, your original $100 will have earned $40 in interest income. However, with a compound interest rate of 4 percent, you will have earned $48.20. Over time, this adds up to a lot more!

Other Savings Options

Besides the savings account, there are a few other ways that your bank can help you put aside some funds for the future. A CD, or certificate of deposit, is similar to a savings account, except typically the bank pays a higher rate of interest. The only catch is that you have to keep your money invested for a specific amount of time. This can be anywhere from a few months to several years. When this period of time ends, you, the investor, may withdraw your money and the interest it has earned. Or, you have the option to "roll it over," or allow it to continue accruing (building up) interest. Some banks charge a penalty fee if you withdraw your money before the time is up. While this isn't the best option for everybody, it is an excellent way to put aside money for college or to protect money for your life after you graduate and begin to look for a job.

Another option you might be interested in is to purchase a savings bond. You can buy a savings bond for as little as $50. Interest is compounded every six months. After thirty years, the bond matures, or stops accruing interest. Then, you take the bond to the bank and withdraw your money, plus interest. While thirty years may seem a long way off now, it's never too early to start safely putting money aside for the future.

Everyone has different reasons for wanting to put aside money for the future. And the good news is that there is a savings method for everyone. Since there are so many options, sometimes the best thing to do is to talk to a banker and ask questions.

three

HOW DO I MANAGE MY PERSONAL MONEY?

The National Foundation for Consumer Credit estimates that 40 percent of middle-class families spend more than they make. It will not be unusual to find yourself in debt at some point in your life. Debt can arise from poor planning, excessive spending, emergencies, or even your decision to buy a necessary big-ticket item that you could not purchase otherwise. For most people, though, debt does not have to last forever.

Here are some hints for reducing credit debt in a personal budget:

Put aside a certain amount of money every payday, or every month if you don't have a job with regular paydays. Open a special bank account if necessary. Use this money for credit card debt reduction only.

Charge it! In the United States, personal credit card debt exceeds $750 billion, accounting for more than one-third of all consumer debt.

→ Place your credit cards in a place where they are not readily available.

→ If you plan to charge an expensive item to a credit card and pay for it over a long period, choose a card with a low interest rate. Obtain a second credit card to use for purchases that will be paid off monthly. With this system, only the one large purchase will incur a monthly finance charge.

→ Call your credit card company and ask about reduced interest rates. Companies can sometimes offer you a better rate if you make payments reliably.

Spending Power

What if you have money left over after all monthly expenses are paid? Economists call this discretionary income. Having excess money indicates that the budget is balanced.

Another way to consider this extra money is as "spending power." Think of it as money that you have the power to spend (or save). It is money that you have a choice about. If you spend more money each month than you receive in income, your spending power is negative. If you make more money each month than you spend, your spending power is positive and you can decide what to do with the excess. Saving money allows spending power to remain high for each month.

Spending power doesn't depend on how much money a person makes; it depends on what the person considers essential needs. As income grows, people often change what they consider essential. One person may consider a large-screen color television a necessity, whereas another would consider it a luxury. The way you define your wants and needs determines how much spending power is available in your budget. On the other hand, you may decide that you want to put some of your discretionary income into a savings account. Saving money allows spending power to remain high for each month. It can also heighten spending power in future months because there will be surplus money in an account. That money will be earning interest, which also increases your spending power.

After setting up a basic personal budget, you may want to adjust it to increase your spending power. Just reevaluate what is necessary. There are two areas in a basic budget that may be adjusted: income and expense.

Spend Less

Many people have items in their budget that they can do without. Therefore, cutting back on expenses is often an easy way to increase spending power. Some ideas for cutting expenses can be started immediately:

New clothes are nice but expensive. Your money will go further if you shop at vintage clothing stores, thrift shops, and secondhand stores.

- Take lunch to school or work instead of eating out.
- Buy less expensive clothing or shop at secondhand stores.
- Use a public or school library as an alternative to renting videos or buying books, tapes, and compact discs.
- Before you go shopping, check the newspaper for special sales. And while you are out shopping, keep your eye out for unadvertised sales or markdowns.
- Buy items in large quantities. For example, buying at a wholesale store can often earn you a discount.
- Be smart about shopping in general. Comparing prices at different stores, bargain hunting, searching for rebates, and clipping coupons can all help cut down your expenses.

Some Other Ways to Save

There are also ways for you to save a little money now that can benefit you in the future. Have you ever considered making your own clothing? Or learning how to make small repairs to your own car? Or refurbishing a piece of old furniture rather than buying something new? All of these things may help you down the road as you develop skills for a possible career, and they save you a little money now.

Earn More

Increasing income is the second method of increasing spending power. Often it takes longer to increase income than to decrease spending. Some options for increasing income in a personal budget include the following:

➡ Find a part-time job. House painting or babysitting may be possibilities.

➡ Ask for a raise in your current pay.

➡ Invest in more education or training. Vocational schools offer training programs that take less than four years to complete. Having a degree or specific training can increase your earning power.

➡ Take night classes at a community college. It will take more time to earn your degree going at night than going full time, but you can make money as you work toward it.

➡ Do odd jobs or landscaping in your neighborhood. There is always someone who is willing to pay for someone else to mow their lawn, walk the dog, or help with other chores.

➡ Are you really good in a particular class? Offer to tutor other students.

➡ Have a yard sale, or sell some items on eBay.

When it comes to finding ways to earn money, be creative! Make a list of your talents and hobbies—maybe you can use one of them to create an income. If you can sew, offer to adjust clothing or make curtains. Do you like gardening? Offer to plant some flowers for a neighbor.

To get started in your search, post an ad in your local newspaper or on a community-oriented Web site like Craigslist.com. Take a look at want ads, too. Perhaps the best thing you can do is to network, or talk to people about what you are trying to do. You may be surprised by how many people will want to help you out.

It's great to be your own boss. Cutting lawns and raking leaves are time-honored ways for suburban teens to make extra cash.

Putting Budgeting Skills to Use

Participation in school activities can be an opportunity to learn and practice budgeting skills. One consideration is that budgeting doesn't always just involve money. Money is one of many resources that may be allocated, or distributed. Budgeting may also involve allocating time, space, materials, and even people (human resources). For example, you might want to start a club for students interested in in-line skating. Your initial budget may look something like this:

Expenses

Photocopying posters to advertise meetings
   $10 per meeting
Refreshments at meetings
   $10 per meeting
Other Needs
   Room for meetings (classroom to be used for about one
       hour after school one night per week)
   Club adviser (volunteer who can donate about two hours
       per month)

Learning good budgeting skills to use at school and at home will help you improve the organizations in which you are involved. Just as important, budgeting skills can be applied to other areas. One of these areas is your job.

Myths and Facts

Saving money is dependent on income.
Fact ➥ No matter how much you make, you can save money. In order to save money, you simply have to spend less than you make.

Shopping during sales saves money Fact ➥ If you really needed the item, then you are saving money. However, sales often tempt you to buy things you otherwise wouldn't purchase, and in greater quantity. And you usually buy twice as much because it is on sale. So you haven't saved any money.

If you make more money, it will be easier to save money. Fact ➥ Making more money than you currently earn does not equate into more savings. If you get a raise and increase your spending, then you will not be saving money. Many people increase their spending, not their savings, with an increase in pay.

You have to be in debt to budget. Fact ➡ A budget can help you get out of debt; however, you don't need to be in debt to budget your money. A budget can help you save money.

 A budget means you will have to spend extra hours doing paperwork. Fact ➡ Once you have your budget set up, paying your bills and knowing where to spend your money can take very little time.

chapter four

HOW CAN I USE MY BUDGETING SKILLS AT WORK?

Working for an employer almost always requires the ability to understand a budget. People working in business use budgets for organizing resources and time. For example, a chef who manages a large kitchen in a restaurant uses a food budget to analyze the variables that go into producing a meal. The cost of producing meals (based on the price of ingredients), the price that can be charged per meal, and the expected volume of business are all analyzed. After considering all the variables, the chef will be able to tell if the restaurant will make a profit. If not, the chef will adjust one of the budget items (probably either the prices the restaurant charges or the cost of ingredients) until a profit can be made.

Other jobs use budgets to allocate people and time. Personnel managers assess the human resource needs of a company and adjust hiring after consulting a personnel budget. These managers have a budget that tells them what amount of money is available for salaries. Even if a job is not at a managerial level, the ability to allocate money and resources is a basic skill needed to succeed in a job today.

Even as a part-time employee, you'll stand out if you have effective budgeting skills. Your boss may give you a project that requires the allocation of money or resources. For example, if you have a job at a frozen yogurt store, you may be required to keep track of how much of each flavor of frozen yogurt is left. If you notice that there is usually peanut butter frozen yogurt left over, but the raspberry is always running low, then the amounts of yogurt that are ordered need to be adjusted. The store's resources are not being used effectively. It is spending the same amount on peanut butter and raspberry frozen yogurt, while the raspberry sells out and the peanut butter goes to waste.

People who are self-employed also use business budgets. A house painter uses a budget to determine costs for a job. If too much money is spent on supplies and the job runs over budget, the painter will not show a profit and will soon be out of business.

The steps for a basic business budget are similar to those of a basic personal budget. They are:

1. Determining and/or understanding a business plan
2. Estimating costs
3. Establishing prices
4. Estimating volume of business

A house painter who orders too much paint for a job will end up losing money. Budgeting skills help businesspeople to keep costs in line with income.

Understanding Business Plans

A business plan is an outline of the goals of a business. Business plans detail what products or services are to be supplied and how much money and resources will be needed. Self-employed people make their own business plans. People who are employed by others may not necessarily know much about the company's business plan, but they need to understand its goals in order to succeed in their jobs.

Teen entrepreneurs usually operate a business that offers a service such snow shoveling, dog walking, or babysitting. If you are an entrepreneur, you might not need to use a formal business plan. An entrepreneur is someone who organizes and operates his or her own business. While businesses such as these do not offer products for sale, they are usually inexpensive to run. For example, if you operate a snow shoveling business, your only expense would likely be a shovel. Luckily for you, this expense would not cut into your earnings too much. So if you spent $10 on a shovel and made $100 shoveling driveways, then you would have made a $90 profit.

Estimating Costs

Some businesses and jobs cost very little to run. Babysitting requires few costs. The babysitter needs only transportation to the job. Others, such as carpet cleaning, have higher costs. Carpet cleaners require special equipment, cleaning supplies, and transportation for their equipment. Not all business costs are alike. To estimate the costs of running a business, a budget must divide costs into two categories: fixed costs and variable costs.

Fixed costs are business expenses that do not change, or that change very little, from month to month. A permanent fixed cost is an expense you expect to pay only once. Materials and equipment needed to run a business are considered fixed costs: equipment specific to the business (such as a carpet

When starting a business, you have to spend money up-front to make money on the back end. The up-front expenses for a dog grooming service would be the cost of your clippers, combs, and other equipment.

cleaning machine for a carpet cleaner) and office equipment are examples. Telephone bills and advertising expenses may be considered fixed costs if they are constant from month to month.

Variable costs are expenses that change from month to month, depending on the volume of business. In other words, variable costs depend on the number of products you sell or the number of customers you have. For example, cleaning fluids for the carpet cleaner are variable costs. This is because the amount that a business uses in a month depends on the number of customers it has that month. The ice cream that a restaurant orders is also a variable cost—the amount varies from month to month based on the amount of ice cream that is consumed.

Establishing Prices

After a company or businessperson determines how much it costs to conduct business, a price must be set for the services or product. There are two common methods for setting prices. The first method is to base prices on what competing businesses charge. For example, if you started your own typing service, it would be a good idea to call other established typing services to see what they charge. When comparing businesses and prices charged, it would be important for you to make sure that the businesses and services offered are comparable. Some typing services charge per word, and some might charge per document.

The second method considers costs and what profit is desired. If you were to choose this method for setting prices

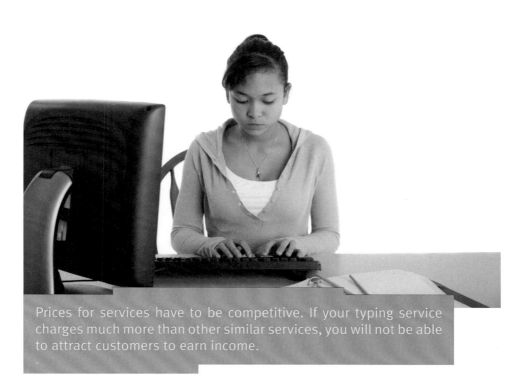

Prices for services have to be competitive. If your typing service charges much more than other similar services, you will not be able to attract customers to earn income.

for your typing service, you would answer the following questions:

Question 1. How much do you want to earn per hour? This is an estimate of an hourly wage.

Question 2. How long does it take to complete each job, make each product, or service each customer?

Question 3. What are the total variable costs per customer? (This amount was determined in the previous budget step.)

Armed with answers to these questions, the typist would be able to set prices for the new typing service by using the following formula:

___ Hours per customer (answer #2)

x (multiplied by)

___ Hourly wage (answer #1)

= (equals)

___ Total wage

Total wage would then be added to total variable costs (answer #3).

___ Total wage

+ (plus)

___ Total variable costs (answer #3)

= (equals)

___ Price

Then, the typist would divide that price by the number of hours per customer (answer #2) to determine the hourly price of the new typing service.

___ Price

÷ (divided by)
___ Hours per customer (answer #2)

= (equals)

___ Hourly price

Estimating Expected Volume of Business

The final step of building a business budget is to estimate how much business is expected. The level of activity a business shows may vary from month to month. Some businesses don't show a profit every month, and their budgets should reflect this. But if a business should earn a certain amount of money each month and does not do so, the budget can be adjusted, often before the company is in trouble.

Let's say that you do not plan to work during the summer months. Since you have planned for this time off, your expected volume of business will be zero for three months of the year.

Putting It All Together

Organizing a business budget takes thought and energy, but it is essential for starting or maintaining a business. Just as with personal budgets, business budgets require updating and adjustment. Price changes for variable costs, increased

Some teens prefer to spend the summer working on their tans instead of their jobs. This time off must be factored into a business budget.

competition, and growth of a business all require budget adjustments.

If you make the effort to learn good budgeting habits, you will be able to apply them to your place of work. For example, you will be able to set long-range plans so that you can achieve your greater goals. Regardless of what kind of job you have, budgeting skills will help you get ahead. You can experience the positive effects now and in your future career.

Ten Great Questions to Ask Yourself About Budgeting

1 How can keeping a budget help me if my income is small?

2 Should I budget my allowance?

3 What are four steps to making a budget?

4 Why do I need a goal for budgeting?

5 How can a worksheet help in budgeting?

6 How is a business budget like a personal budget?

7 Would budgeting help me if I owned my own business?

8 Would a budget be useful if I had a family of my own?

9 How can a budget help me to get out of debt?

10 Why can credit cards cause trouble if I don't keep a budget?

Glossary

accrue To accumulate or be added to periodically.

allocate To set something aside for a special purpose.

balanced budget Budget in which the amount of money received or earned is equal to or greater than the amount of money spent.

big-ticket item Term used to describe something with a high price.

budget Plan that helps control how and where money is spent; a financial map.

business plan Written outline of a business idea including money needed, goals, and a plan to reach those goals.

certificate of deposit (CD) Savings certificate entitling the bearer to receive interest.

compound interest Interest paid on the original principal as well as on the accumulated past interest.

credit history (credit report) Record of an individual's past borrowing and repaying.

debt An obligation or liability to pay something to someone else.

depositor One who puts money in a bank.

discretionary income The amount of money left over after all necessities are paid for.

expense Money spent by a person or business.

financial goal Something that you plan to do with your money, such as buy a car.

fixed expenses Expenses that are the same each month.

income Money that you earn or that is given to you, most commonly for doing some kind of work; the profit a business earns.

interest A charge for money borrowed.

long-term goals Tasks you want to accomplish within a long period of time—a week, a month, or a year.

luxuries Items that you can live without.

necessities Items that you cannot live without; food is a necessity.

profit Amount of money earned in a business after the costs of producing and selling its product are paid.

short-term goal Task you want to accomplish within a short period of time.

spending power Extra money that one has the power to spend as one chooses.

spreadsheet program Computer program that arranges information, often financial data, in a table.

statement Summary of activity issued by a credit card company or other financial institution.

The Consumer Credit Counseling Service (CCCS)
9009 West Loop South, Suite 700
Houston, TX 77096
(713) 923-2227
Web site: http://www.cccsintl.org
The Consumer Credit Counseling Service (CCCS) provides
services to individuals who are struggling with debt and
personal budgeting problems. This nonprofit organization's
services include helping people create personal budgets
and negotiating with creditors. Look in the telephone
directory in the white pages business section. CCCS has
offices in most major cities.

The Future Business Leaders of America
1912 Association Drive
Reston, VA 20191
(800) FBLA-WIN (325-2946)
Web site: http://www.fbla-pbl.org
The Future Business Leaders of America offers services
that promote self-confidence, leadership, and business
skills, such as budgeting. Contact the national head-
quarters to find out if a local chapter exists in your area.

National Council on Economic Education

1140 Avenue of the Americas

New York, NY 10036

(212) 730-7007

(800) 338-1192

Web site: http://www.ncee.net

  The National Council on Economic Education has programs
  to help students apply what they learn in school to their lives.

U.S. Department of Commerce

1401 Constitution Avenue NW

Washington, DC 20230

(202) 482-2000

Web site: http://www.commerce.gov

  The mission of the Department of Commerce is to foster,
  promote, and develop domestic commerce. This mission
  includes assisting communities and individuals with economic
  progress.

U.S. Small Business Administration (SBA)

6302 Fairview Road, Suite 300

Charlotte, NC 28210

(800) UASK-SBA (817-5722)

Web site: http://www.sba.gov

  The U.S. Small Business Administration (SBA) offers programs
  and services to help businesspeople with budgets. The SBA
  can provide training, educational programs, publications, and
  advice. The SBA has offices around the country.

Web Sites

Due to the changing nature of Internet links, Rosen Publishing has developed an online list of Web sites related to the subject of this book. This site is updated regularly. Please use this link to access the list:

http://www.rosenlinks.com/faq/bamm

For Further Reading

Bowman-Khrum, Mary. *Money: Save It, Manage It, Spend It*. Berkley Heights, NJ: Enslow Publishers, 2000.

Brain, Marshall. *The Teenager's Guide to the Real World*. Raleigh, NC: BYG Publishing, 1997.

Burkett, Larry, with Todd Temple. *Money Matters Workbook for Teens (Ages 15–18)*. Chicago, IL: Moody Press, 1998.

Carson, Doc. *Gone Shopping! An Odyssey of Discovery*. Lecompton, KS: High Way Publishing, 2004.

Deering, Kathryn R. *Cash and Credit Information for Teens*. Detroit, MI: Omnigraphics, Inc., 2005.

Dvorkin, Howard S. *Credit Hell: How to Dig Out of Debt*. New York, NY: John Wiley & Sons, 2005.

Gardner, David, and Tom Gardner. *The Motley Fool Investment Guide for Teens*. New York, NY: Fireside Publishers, 2002.

Godfrey, Neal S. *Ultimate Kids' Money Book*. New York, NY: Aladdin, 2002.

Ireland, Susan. *The Complete Idiot's Guide to Cool Jobs for Teens*. Royersford, PA: Alpha, 2001.

Khalfani, Lynnette. *Zero Debt: The Ultimate Guide to Financial Freedom*. South Orange, NJ: Advantage World Press, 2004.

Orman, Suze. *The Money Book for the Young, Fabulous & Broke*. New York, NY: Penguin Group, 2006.

Pervola, Cindy, and Debby Hobgood. *How to Get a Job if You're a Teenager*. Fort Atkinson, WI: Upstart Books, 2000.

Richards, Kristi. *Making, Managing, and Milking Your Money: What Every Teen Needs to Know*. Charleston, SC: BookSurge Publishing, 2003.

Shelly, Susan. *Complete Idiot's Guide to Money for Teens*. Royersford, PA: Alpha Publishing, 2001.

Valliant, Doris. *Personal Finance* (Exploring Business and Economics). New York, NY: Chelsea House, 2001.

index

About the Author

Matt Monteverde is a writer currently living in Summit, New Jersey. In addition to this book, he has written books for teens focusing on such crucial issues as addictive gambling and teenage violence. He earned a bachelor's degree in sociology from Rutgers University in 2003.

Photo Credits

Cover © www.istockphoto.com/Winston Davidian; pp. 5, 7, 25, 52 Shutterstock.com; p. 8 © Scott Olson/Getty Images; p. 10 © www.istockphoto.com/Jason Stitt; p. 13 © Ellen B. Senisi/The Image Works; p. 16 © The Copyright Group/SuperStock; p. 19 © www.istockphoto.com/Chase Swift; p. 22 © Michael Krasowitz/Taxi/Getty Images; p. 29 © Arnold Gold/New Haven Register/The Image Works; p. 34 © www.istockphoto.com/Ilya Genkin; p. 36 © Bob Daemmrich/The Image Works; p. 39 © www.istockphoto.com/Randolph Pamphrey; p. 45 © www.istockphoto.com/Linda Macpherson; p. 47 © www.istockphoto.com/olga zaporozhskaya; p. 49 © www.istockphoto.com/Ana Abejon.

Designer: Evelyn Horovicz; Photo Researcher: Amy Feinberg